CW00402138

Harmonica

First Edition

ISBN 1-903110-11-4

Cover Design Owen Benwell

Published in 2003 by
Wrecking Ball Press
9 Westgate • North Cave • Brough • East Yorkshire • HU15 2NG

Geoff Hattersley

HARMONICA

Acknowledgements

...are due to the following magazines and anthologies, where some of these poems, or earlier versions of them, first appeared:

The Reater, The Yellow Crane, The North, Headlock, Billy Liar, The Echo Room Yearbook, The Penniless Press, Scratch, Prop, Fat City, Moodswing, Pennine Platform, Liar Republic, and *Gosh! Poetry!*

For Jeanette Hattersley
my family and friends

Contents I

Contents II

Contents III

I

I Was an Unarmed Teenager

Sunday morning, just after nine
or just before, and the Salvation Army band
strike up a dirge
right under the window.
I roll my hangover
from one red eye to the other, sit up
and stare down at the musicians
in their uniforms, rasping
their dirty hankie tune -
I shoot them
through their mouthpieces
with an imaginary gun.

My mother's getting warm
in front of an open oven,
a pot of tea just made,
Sunday People on the table
open at the crossword page,
and the dog slobbers toward me
with prisoner's eyes
but he's no chance
of a walk on the canal bank
right now. "How do you die
like a cowboy," my mother asks,
"four-three-four?"

Before And After Breakfast

I have to check the furniture
hasn't moved round during the night,
that the bathroom mirror's still broken -
there's a lot of stuff to get done
before breakfast, including forgetting
the dream where I was patronised
across a shiny desk that stretched for miles
by some know-nowt who believes
his life amounts to something.

I go to fetch some bread and milk,
the pavement's full of holes...
I'm wondering what there is
to look forward to.
Breakfast, I guess, and after that,
a film on at midnight -
I've seen it a good few times
but it's worth watching again.
Henry Fonda bites the dust
with a harmonica in his mouth.
You can't help thinking about it,
you can even take it seriously.

Jumbo

I'm not skinny
but this bloke next to me
in the fish 'n' chip shop
makes me look it.
He fondles a roll of
mucky tenners,
slides one out
to pay for his chips 'n' jumbo.
Then this woman glides in
like a slow cat
and the fat bloke winks at me
and says to her,
'Sorry Love, I just bought
the last jumbo sausage.'
He holds it out
right in her face.
'Don't worry,' she says,
peering at it
then meeting the bloke's eyes,
'I've another one just like it
waiting for me when I get home.'
And he's the one who ends up
blushing.

Walking home, eating chips
with my fingers,
I see an empty can
and score a perfect goal.

Cold Spot

I've taken to wearing
a jacket in the house,
it's colder than outside,
the walls are damp,
dripping sometimes,
this is a dump alright,
where I live, fastened in
with the noise of cars
and lorries streaming past,
in my head like harsh voices
or bad music, my breath
steaming up the window
as I stand watching
people without cars,
old, slow, cold, hanging on,
keeping death away
with whatever it takes
and their shopping bags.

I flush the toilet,
hear next door's baby
start to cry. I stand
and listen. It cries and
cries and cries.

Smoke

The first time I lit up in front of him
it was about midnight,
I was watching The Marx Brothers with Dave.
I was fifteen, Dave was thirteen,
my dad must have been thirty-eight.
I was gagging for a No. 6,
willing my dad to fall asleep
in the chair like he often did.
I think the film was *Room Service*;
something they weren't at their best in.
I stared. I got more and more tense.
In the end I just lit a fag
like it was the most natural thing
in the world for me to do
and my dad
stood very slowly,
walked out and up the stairs
without a word
for months.

The Slacker

for David Kennedy

All he's done this summer
is play with dice.
The work was abandoned
like a flat pint.
All he's done is listen
to nobodies
and try to understand
nothing at all.

It's 10 a.m., Sunday
in an old town
where the church bells
won't stay quiet for long.
He's there like chewing gum
stuck to a shoe,
an old brown shoe
in an airless attic.

He stares irresolute
at his bookshelves.
There aren't any new books
he wants to read.
There aren't any old ones
he could re-read.
He selects one
but just can't open it.

Two Love Poems

(i) Younger, Fresher

I got my hair cut
this morning, too short
is how it looks to me
but she likes it, Jeanette.
She says it makes me look
younger, fresher.
She says it makes me look
as if I know I'm living a life
that could be
much worse.
"Do you like them?" she asks,
turning her feet this way and that
in some new black
high-heeled sandals.

(ii) Bed Poem

She holds me from behind
or I curl up to her,
I like to feel her warm
backside. Like a workman's
brazier, I tell her.
Go to sleep, she murmurs.

I'm sure someone once said
a poem should be like an
onion, peeling it, layer after layer
bringing tears to the eyes,
but who'd want to wake up
in bed with that person?

Splinter
i.m. Mona Eileen Hattersley, 1935-1998

She said it was too small for her to see
and too small for my dad to see
but she had a splinter in her finger,

it was driving her up the wall -
this was when she was about fifty-five
so I was about thirty-four.

She passed me a pair of tweezers,
told me to take the splinter out
if I could see it. I could see it alright

and I got it with the tweezers
and pulled it straight out, no messing,
and my mother gave a sigh of relief.

Eight years later she was full of cancer,
drugged up, surrounded by cards and flowers,
fussed over by strangers in uniforms.

We took her home for the last month, she insisted.
'They can't make a proper cup of tea here,' she said,
'it's no wonder everybody's badly.'

My Shoes Need Cleaning

I am the ultimate slacker,
it says so in a review

written by a man who puts Dr.
at the front of his name.

And then I stuff the magazine
in the bin and wonder

if I should cut my fingernails
or merely roll a cigarette.

I do work for a living, though.
Nobody there calls me Dr.,

nobody calls themselves Dr.
I guess nobody's a Dr.

The 41 Greatest Lists of 41

41 Excuses That Were Never Used
The 41 Greatest Chapter Twos
41 Catchphrases To Make Thee Titter
41 Scotsmen With A Chip On Their Shoulder
41 Famous People With Size Sixteen Feet
41 Dead Men Who Used To Eat Meat
41 Aviators Who Were Scared Of Flying
41 Politicians Who Were Caught Out Lying
41 Picassos That Turned Out To Be Fake
41 Geniuses Who Disappeared Without A Trace
41 Ways To Make A Fool See Sense
The Top 41 Clowns Living In Tents
41 People Who Forgot To Check The Loopholes
41 Men Who Chose Not To Have Balls
The 41 Best Inner Sleeves of 1974
41 People Who Went Through The Green Door
My Favourite 41 One-Armed Drummers
41 Places To Avoid In The Summer
41 Plumbers Who Can't Fix A Leak
41 Species That Will Be Extinct Next Week
41 Practical Jokes That Ended In Grief
41 Popular Phrases To Express Disbelief
41 Actors Who Forgot the Script
41 Builders Whose Jeans Actually Fit
41 Policemen Who Died Of Mirth
41 Texans Who Should Have Been Drowned At Birth
41 Country Singers With A Broken Heart
41 Country Singers Who Broke A Different Part
41 Items Never Found Anywhere Except In A Dustbin
41 Unusual Places To Wear A Safety-Pin
The 41 Step Guide To Walking Down The Street
41 Goalkeepers Who Never Kept A Clean Sheet
41 Instructions You Must Follow To The Letter
41 Diseases That Won't Get Any Better
41 Candles on the Child Star's Birthday Cake
41 Women Who Were Burnt At The Stake
41 Ways To Enjoy Vodka and Orange
41 Ways To Enjoy Gin and Orange
41 Ways To Enjoy Whiskey and Orange
41 Poets Who Couldn't Chew What They'd Bitten
41 Lines That Should Never Have Been Written

Randy Newman et al

The five greatest living American Jewish songwriters
have been in my ears most of the weekend,
they make me feel like chewing my arm off

and that never hurt anyone.
The sixth greatest would have been in my ears as well
only I'm not sure who it is. Maybe Neil Diamond...

The weather is nothing like a woman
or the weather is exactly like a woman.
I suppose it depends on the woman.

I can hardly believe I'm forty-two.
I feel fifteen or twenty-six or thirty-eight
but never forty-two or forty-one.

Harmonica

The world continues to be mad,
at times seeming to deteriorate
much faster, suddenly worse than ever

and accepted that way, humoured.
In the privacy of his home
he is mad too, playing Chicago blues

on a crappy harmonica
in a shirt he's worn for seventeen days.
He plays the blues till he's done for

then eats some cold pieces of pie, pork pie
and apple pie. No one hears him laughing
at least he doesn't think so.

Before and After Midnight

Wasn't *The Doors* a bloody stupid film?
I just laughed my head off at it.
I don't think I've ever liked a film less.

The telly's off, I smoke a cigarette.
Elsewhere, people rip pieces out of each other
in broken rooms that stink,

beer and pig's breath... I decide to phone Nev
in Sweden, years of long-distance friendship
hanging between us like frayed ropes.

We're not in control of our destinies -
how the fuck did I end up here?
he says, I think, something like that.

Nineteen or Twenty Pigeons

This bright morning in his new apartment
he loves the sunlight striking everything,
smoke from his cigarette rising through it.

If he knew what was expected of him
he'd surely achieve it, a day like this,
alive and well behind the huge windows.

He stares at the pigeons on the rooftop
of the bakery below, tries to count them.
He wipes sleep from his eyes though he's already washed.

He can clearly recall a hot summer
when he looked like a corpse and felt like one.
All he desires is a boiled egg sandwich.

The Plan

I had a plan, of sorts, listen to this -
I'd get myself nailed to a wooden plank
like the saddest bastard who ever lived.

I was crazy no doubt, but how crazy
do you have to be before people realise?
There were crazier people on the loose.

I was proud of my plan, it seemed enough.
I was trying hard to concentrate
but my mind kept drifting off

to imaginary punk blues anthologies
and metaphysical Western movies,
sometimes starring Burt Lancaster.

His Chilling Thought

At least his boat had come in money-wise.
At least he didn't have to work any more.
At least he'd been spared that.

At least he was living:
he could steam the windows up with his smoky breath
which was all the proof he needed.

At least he wasn't a washed-up country singer.
At least he had no less than six good pairs of shoes.
In fact, these really should have been

the best days of his life, the happiest.
Perhaps they were; it was a chilling thought
that un-nerved him as he buttered some toast.

At This Table

I stare at the letter. It's from a young poet
who wants advice on how to get gigs in New York,
as if I could help him, barefoot and hungover

at this table in Huddersfield, up to my neck in shit.
This was meant to be my way out.
I'm laughing my head off the more I think of it.

I've been staying out of the sun, I get cold sores.
You have to avoid intimate oral contact,
where's the fun in that... Now Jeanette's telling me

about all the shopping trolleys in the canal
and on the bottom, plastic traffic cones.
The ducks appear unruffled however.

Her New Biker

He grins through his stubble
and offers her another line
and she's not somebody who'd turn it down

because it's good to feel stronger, less real
and break the harsh routine
for a short while.

She plays the new album
by The Red Hot Chili Peppers
to make him feel at home

and sets a mug of steaming tea
on the table, next to his crash helmet
and gloves and paraphernalia.

Unrecalled Melody

How come I feel like a blues guitarist
for whom the music has grown stale,
who can't recall the melody he was whistling

when he started the day with a glass of whiskey,
who always talks about himself in the past tense?
It's one a.m., very quiet,

it's hot, my head is hot, my hands.
I sit at the table with the lights off,
there are three huge windows to look out of.

There are places where people are working,
illuminated like poultry farms.
People dying, listen, begging for life.

Her Question

"Now what are we going to do?"
She'd asked the same question
till she was sick of saying it.

He kicked a small stone, sending it
twenty yards; a good shot,
he thought, bloody good shot.

He reached out to hold her hand then.
"I don't know," he replied,
"what we're going to do."

He was all out of ideas.
He'd lifted the lid, found the jar empty.
He'd poked around in it and there was nothing there.

II

A Terrible Song

was just starting. I switched it off
and went to buy a loaf. I had the usual
small worries, sleeplessness
and being at the mercy of dentists,
fourteen hundred tons of job
and the chance I might drop dead
before crawling out from under it,
the possibility of reincarnation
as a business man's fat cigar,
forever puffed on half-smoked in mean lips.
Like someone trying to escape through a porthole
getting their backside stuck, that's how
I felt, and that's not all, there was
a fresh bunch of flowers
tied to the bus stop down the street
again, a fresh bunch of flowers
is tied to the bus stop every Sunday.
I don't know why, I don't know
if I want to know. I don't know much
these days, but I do at least know
a terrible song when I hear one.

Small Chocolate Heart

Estimated Cycle Time:
58.8 seconds

The press opens
I open the gate
remove the mould
I spray the tool
shut the gate
I push the green button
the press closes
I trim the mould
I pack the mould

Instructions To Operator:
Remove Feedgates Flush
Check Each Shot For
Pulling And Plucking

The press opens
I open the gate
remove the mould
I spray the tool
shut the gate
I push the green button
the press closes
I trim the mould
I pack the mould

It's ten in the morning
sunny and warm outside
I'm wearing tight shoes

The press opens
I open the gate
remove the mould
I spray the tool
shut the gate
I push the green button
the press closes
I trim the mould
I pack the mould

Remember: The Next Inspection
Is By The Customer

The press opens
I open the gate
remove the mould
I spray the tool
shut the gate
I push the green button
the press closes
I trim the mould
I pack the mould

Nine hours fifty-six minutes
four point eight seconds
to go

The press opens

The Depth

Management. Two of them
and a couple of young lackeys
are in my way for half an hour
discussing the depth of the mould
coming out of the LB350
every 47.9 seconds.
"They won't wear it. I know
they won't."
"But anything less and it would
fall off."
I stop listening, try to carry on
as if they're not
present, as if I'm not,
as if I was under a parachute
gliding in a blue sky.
Then they are gone.
Our Quality Control Inspector
strides over.
"And what pearls of wisdom
did that lot have for you?"
They were talking, I tell him, about
the depth of the mould.
"The depth?" he says. "*The depth*?"
He turns, walks back to his office
shaking his head.
"They haven't got
a clue. Haven't got
a buggerin' clue."

It's the sort of job where you lose
something, something
you spend the weekends
looking for with tired eyes.

Two Hours And One Minute

10.57 a.m.

Someone lobs a sprue at me
across the top of some boxes,
missing my head by inches.
I think it was Frank.
It could have been Orville.

12.13 p.m.

I open my bag
to get a banana;
it's been stuffed
with corrugated cardboard,
empty crisp packets,
used plastic cups,
etc.

12.19 p.m.

Jacko appears
right in my face:
"If you *ever*
do anything like that again
I'll pull your bollocks off."
I watch him walk away.
I don't know what I did.

12.58 p.m.

I spot Orville
leaning across a stillage;
I grab a sweeping brush,
cross forty yards in no time,
and jab him up the arse
with the handle.

Cowboy

No one's quite sure how old he is
and he doesn't let on
but my guess is sixty-one.
He's worked here all his life, he says,
since he was seventeen,
"and I haven't got a pot to piss in."
He wears cowboy boots and thick leather belts,
blasts country 'n' western
from his cassette player all day.
"Yee-ha!" the others shout, "Yee-ha!"
He just grins, keeps quiet
like a grey-haired outlaw
with nothing left to prove.

One morning he asks me
what a paedophile is.
"Go away," I mutter.
I walk over, tell Frank.
"Hey," Frank shouts, "Cowboy,
what's all this about you
becoming a paedophile then?"

Powder Man

"Fuck off!" he shouts.
"Get fucked!" I shout back.
It's how Jacko and I
say hello every day,
it keeps him happy
and amuses me too.
He's the powder man
who keeps the machines going,
it's a back-breaking job.
He prowls the factory
with a head full of films
like *Full Metal Jacket*,
punching things as he goes,
people if he's that way out.
In a U.S. Marine haircut
he'll say, "Outta the way, Buddy."
His neck's thicker
than some girls' waists.
"I'd shag any woman,"
he informs me,
"except for one."
He doesn't say
which one.

Humphrey Bogart

How do you get through life
without knowing who Humphrey Bogart is?
I've been thinking about him for weeks
and mention him to Gary
while we're walking to work.
"Humphrey What?" he says.
I laugh, can hardly believe it,
but it turns out he won't watch anything
on the telly in black and white.
So I tell him Bogart
was Rick, Sam Spade, Marlowe, Harry Morgan,
that he was a guy with lines
and knew how they needed to be said.
He likes that, and takes off his dark glasses
to show me a black eye,
tells me him and his mates
got in a scrap Saturday night,
that he started it, just simply
thumped some geezer without warning.
Why'd you do that? I ask.
"He was a fatso. I don't like fatsos."

No Chance

It's summer, and I stare
from where I'm stuck
trimming moulds for chocolate dog bones
across the floor at Ken,
who's fifty-seven,
who had a heart attack four years ago
during his dinner break.
There he is at the Fourteen Hundred,
hoisting hot, sharp, heavy fans,
sweat staining the back of his shirt
like a lake on a map, pouring down
his flushed forehead and face
and off the end of his nose.
He shakes his head and a thick spray
flies from his hair.
I can't watch too long, have to look away,
have to get on with my own work
which is just as tough
in this sort of heat.
I think if I had a heart attack
they wouldn't get me back in here
at gunpoint. That's obvious.
I wonder what Ken was scared of
and frown.

Summer Sick Note

We've got lavender toilet paper
made in Worksop
dinner is in the oven
oven is in the kitchen
I'm in the living room
watching the traffic
an endless procession
all sorts of vehicles
here on this road to Blackpool

a young black guy
in a red convertible
his shades reflecting
the bright morning sun
there goes someone with a canoe on their roof
another with a dog at the wheel
and one with a human head
stuck on the bonnet
it's going to be a hot day

my brother Dave is in Sweden
my great friend Nev, he's there as well
I'm not getting much done
watching the traffic from this chair
but it beats the factory
beats it hands down
a bad case of the runs, I told them
it feels great to be here
with no clothes on

Alex

I don't feel great
about the job I do
but I've got to
feel better than Alex.
On the Fourteen Hundred
making TP9 fans -
they're huge, heavy, very hot moulds
you can barely handle -
he suddenly shouts
"I HATE THIS BASTARD JOB!"
then places his hand
palm down on the table
and whacks it hard
with a five-pound hammer.
It's the second time
he's broken a hand.
Previously, he punched
a concrete post.

Bad Attitude

We each took turns
to pick a cardboard box
up off the floor,
take three self-conscious steps
in slow motion
and put it down again,
and six months later
the Works Manager
gave us fancy certificates
saying we'd attended a course
in Manual Handling.
After I'd stopped laughing
the Works Manager told me
I'd a bad attitude;
he stood gaping
like I was something odd;
"but you turn up on time,"
he added, "and do your job,"
and then he smiled
and I smiled
and he walked back to his office.

Ride

To be honest, I didn't care for him,
but was prepared to accept his offer
of a lift home after work in his car.

Talking to him was like selling snails from door to door
so I stopped, listened instead to the latest dance stuff
on his loud radio. I could just about stand it

after the noise of the machines all day,
the minutes and hours gone for good
with the whiff of sweat and the voices of bosses.

Steve was twenty years old and the word was
he'd never done it with a girl.
I smiled and said thanks for the ride.

Spliff

When he wakes up he's forty-one years old
and the heatwave appears to have ended
like a tricky piece of oboe music.

Only seven o'clock and already
the noise of vehicles and industry
and he can't be bothered to wash or shave.

He makes a spliff, mean with the tobacco,
sits and smokes it at the kitchen table.
He's suspecting he'll be late for work

yet feels completely at ease, staring
at the traffic without noticing it
and without it noticing him.

Joy

A young Sikh with a grin drives the taxi.
"I bet there's some joy and rejoicing
going on in there this Sunday morning,"
he says as we arrive. I laugh at that
and pay him and get out, moving
slowly, clock in and go to my machine
where the night shift operator
looks just about ready to climb the wall.
He's something of a smackhead, I've been told,
and I believe it, he's certainly weird.
But who on this planet isn't,
and aren't I working seven till seven
every Saturday and Sunday
and taking taxis to the stinking place?

I've dropped on for an easy job today
but stupidly have brought nothing to read
and have to scrounge round for something. I get
The Sunday Mirror, the *Sport on Sunday*
and Friday's *The Sun*, and I read all three
at great length, God help me, I read all three.

Poem Mentioning Adolph Hitler

This isn't a hard luck story,
though it's true these moulds are so hot
they burn my hands when I touch them
and I'm gasping for a smoke.
This isn't a hard luck story
but I made the mistake of telling Jed
that I didn't like Spurs;
"Adolph didn't like them either," he said
and winked, and it occured to me
it's important to have a good reason
for disliking something.
This isn't a hard luck story
because the afternoon goes quick
with Creedence Clearwater Revival
blasting out from Jimmy's table,
carrying fifty yards,
loud enough to be heard
over ten huge plastic injection moulding machines.
This isn't a hard luck story.
We breathe, we press buttons, we drink coffee,
we sweat and complain and blow our noses.
We're here making money for someone else
and a little for ourselves too.

Y'Know Warramean?

Everything he tells you
he follows with the phrase
Y'know warramean?
He's used to drinking every night
Y'know warramean?
I don't mean he goes out every night
he might just have a few cans in the house
Y'know warramean?
If he could get out of the habit of drinking every night
then he wouldn't have to drink every night
Y'know warramean?
And you feel like grabbing hold of him and shouting
I'M NOT THREE YEARS OLD, OF COURSE I KNOW WHAT YOU MEAN
Y'KNOW WARRAMEAN?
But you don't do that and he carries on
Y'know warramean?

He can't do overtime at the weekends
because of his Community Service
Y'know warramean?
He got done for almost nothing
well they called it assault
Y'know warramean?
I mean you can't call it assault
all he did was shout at her in the street
Y'know warramean?
Well she told the coppers he hit her
Y'know warramean?
Well he might have pushed her slightly
Y'know warramean?
It's o.k., the Community Service
it'd be o.k. if you were getting paid
Y'know warramean?

Boss Arse

I almost got the sack,
I almost thumped a man
for the first time in twenty years,
a short fat strutting man
who thinks he knows who he is
and who I am, but who knows
less than corrugated cardboard
cut into strips, put in a pile,
less than rusty blades in a tin.
I can hardly believe he's real.
I could hardly believe him real
even as I shook my fist in his face -
"Fuck off you fucking little cunt!"
I should have been cooler somehow,
I should have been something like a freezer;
all afternoon I behave like someone
treading round a puddle of oil,
and the odious little man
still exists, scheming
in a brightly-lit office.

Lee's Dog

Lee brought his dog to work
because his dad had gone away
and the dog didn't like
being alone all day.
Christ, I said, it's a dog,
it doesn't have to like it,
what's it going to do,
pack a suitcase and leave?
Lee tethered it
outside the back door, right next
to where he was working
on the reject mouldings
granulating machine.
It was a huge, stupid-looking beast,
just the sort of dog
a halfwit like Lee would go for,
and it lay on its belly
in the sun all day
with its ugly tongue
lolling from its mouth.
Every time I ducked out
for a cigarette
the dog would be there.
I didn't come even close
to liking it
or anything like that.

Race Relations on the Shop Floor

We had a young Asian man start,
he only worked three or four days.

He sliced his thumb pretty badly
trimming lawnmower underdecks.

There was a lot of blood,
all over the table and floor.

I stood looking at it with Lee.
It was our job to clean it up.

Lee said he was surprised there was so much -
“Pakis don’t like to part with owt, do they?”

For a while we had two Asian workers
known to most as “The Quiet Paki”

and “The Gobby Paki”
but they didn’t last long either.

Two Versions of a Cartoon Strip

1

'DON'T DRINK THAT!' the Works Manager shouted
as I took the plastic cup of coffee

out of the machine, raised it to my lips.
I was so shocked I dropped the cup.

'DON'T DRINK THAT BLOODY POISON!' he shouted
and turned and ran away.

I thought he'd finally flipped his lid
and imagined him being bundled out

ranting and raving in a straightjacket.
It was a funny thought, I grinned at it.

2

The Works Manager is in a right flap,
the upper management
furious in their suits.
It seems the drinks machine has been tampered with,
the water tank topped up
with cheap brandy.
I'm loving every minute,
working close enough to the drinks machine
to see everything happening,
but I have to try and look grim.
I try, but can't quite manage it.
"I suppose you find all this amusing,"
the Works Manager snarls.
I should get an award
for not bursting out laughing.

Chicken Bone Charlie

The three lads in the bus station
are just about legless, shouting 'Barmy Army'
over and over
as we wait for the
Marsden Hard End. It's 7.28
on a Saturday evening. I'm on my way home
from work, a hard job made harder today
by the close company of Chicken Bone Charlie,
a scruffy-arsed little ragamuffin
who got on the wrong side of me
first thing in the morning
by playing a 90-minute Meat Loaf cassette
at full volume on his ghetto blaster.
We didn't speak from 7.15 a.m. to 6 p.m.,
despite working side by side. Then I said,
'Only one hour to go,' and he replied,
'Good. I'm sick of having to look at you.'
So I said, 'Even your best friend
must be sick of looking at *you*',
then neither of us
spoke again, as the last hour
dragged its heavy feet.

Things Suddenly Liven Up

There was no first-aid man
the Sunday afternoon
Winston caught his wrist
with his trimming knife.
We wrapped yards of bandage
as tightly as we could
while the supervisor
became hysterical.

The nearest hospital
was Huddersfield. I had to navigate
while the supervisor drove.
We were all over the road.
Poor Winston in the back.
He didn't make a sound
all the way there. Blood still seeped through
the layers of bandage.

We left him in Casualty
and drove back to the job.
The supervisor was stricken
but I couldn't help grinning.
It had been a good hour
of unexpected excitement.

Like Harpo Marx

I spend my time standing in places like this
to make me the money that buys me the things that are
my things once I've bought 'em, not some other fucker's.

You're beaten if you take it home with you -
the job, all the bullshit.
You try to think about something better

but you can't help going back to *the place.*
I just die there, trying hard not to scream,
nodding my head like Harpo Marx.

I found out who it was did me house over.
They're in jail for car theft. Soon as they're out
I'm going to smack six shades of shit out of 'em.

The Handshake Poem

The summer's here, and the Managing Director
has just cleared out his desk, looking shaken
to be sacked for incompetence, and with rumours
of financial shenanigans and back-handers
laughed about openly on the shop-floor.

Last Christmas, he handed me a large box
of Cadbury's Milk Tray and said, glancing
at the name patch on my pale blue workshirt,
"Merry Christmas, Geoff", and shook hands with me
as though we were sealing a weapons deal.

And then, after catching me outside with a fag
when I should have been trimming lawnmower handles,
my first fag for three, nearly four long hours,
he gave me, some time in April or May,
my third written warning for misconduct.

The summer's here, and the Managing Director
has left the premises, his tail between his legs.
"They say he took ten grand from some Germans..."
We're all sure he's guilty, even if they prove him innocent.
Nothing could mar our ebullient mood.

Ongoing

It's strange to stand here
doing the most mundane job invented.
I've become a dab hand
with a very sharp knife.
There's time to fold my arms
and reflect as I wait for the machine
to complete its cycle
on how dull it is to do this.

We're treated like schoolboys.
There's a list of things we can't do.
No smoking. No eating.
No reading. No crosswords.
No lounging on the tables
as it presents a slovenly image
and damages the tables too.
We need permission to go for a piss.

It's strange to stand here
while share prices vacillate
and while marine biologists
eat sandwiches on warm beaches
and while cats stalk sparrows
in overgrown gardens
and while movie stars make movies
that are nothing like life.

I Did Brain Surgery On A Barnsley Pub Floor

Wayne by the juke-box lost an eye at the weekend,
Wayne watching Wayne and Wayne playing pool broke both arms -
he was complaining he couldn't wipe his backside.

Wayne walked in with a dog's skull in the palm of his hand -
"Alas, poor Wayne, my fair sister," he said.
He sat down at the bar, in between Wayne and Wayne.

Wayne proposed a toast to Wayne, but Wayne, Wayne and Wayne
refused to drink and left in a bit of a huff.
"John Wayne films! I bloody well can't stand them!"

shouted Wayne, the uninjured one with the moustache.
I took my scalpel out and introduced myself -
"Hello, I'm a surgeon of some renown, Dr. Wayne..."

Memorable Afternoon at the Cinema

The new director's cut of *The Wild Bunch*
has brought us here, DK and I. It's very good
at making old stuff seem new, and at the end

when the outlaws take on the Mexican soldiers,
imagine our surprise as it becomes clear
bullets are leaving the screen, members of the audience

screaming as chunks of flesh and blood burst from their bodies
in slow motion. We have to throw ourselves to the ground
as a few rounds from Lyle Gorch head our way.

"That Peckinpah!" says DK as we leave,
shaking his head, grinning at all the blood
seeping through the left sleeve of my denim jacket.

His Fingernails

I told him his hands were someone else's,
it was their fingernails he'd been chewing,
but he just laughed, as if I was joking.

So I pulled out a large brown envelope,
photographic evidence and so on,
dropped it on the table in front of him.

He stared at it and then he picked it up.
I tapped my feet and hummed 'Smokestack Lightning'
as he tried to take it all in, and then

he was sobbing and my arm was round him.
There, there, I said, you'll feel better later.
I was lying. He'd never feel better.

Posh

There's certainly been a lot of wine drunk,
most of it by a young man in a suit
strutting about the place like a loud boss -

"Six thousand quid," he bleats, "six thousand quid."
He behaves that way because he's stupid
but stupidity isn't an excuse.

Surely we're not being served lion steaks?
I have to stare again at the packet
as it pokes from the top of the swing bin

and look our hostess's legs up and down
like a cheap hoodlum in a B-movie
as she polishes knobs on her posh new cooker.

The Guitar

I can't stand this guitar. It doesn't like me much either.
It is between my hands like a severed limb.
Sometimes I think my fingers must have been severed.

I'm hanging on to the one chord I know.
I need a drummer like I used to need mother.
I'm kicking the table-legs and stamping.

Sometimes I think I must be aurally impaired.
I know what I like when I hear it though.
The problem is, I don't hear it, that's the problem.

I know this chord by heart. I can play it perfect.
I can play it but I can't get off it.
I'd call Bad Musicians Rescue Service if there was one.

The Phone Call

It would be wrong of me not to make the phone call,
the phone call I promised I would make at this time,
and yet I only stare at the phone, don't use it.

If the phone rang right now I'd collapse in a heap.
I switch the ringer volume off, replace the phone
and sit back and stare at the phone and wonder.

I put some music on but can't hear it for the phone.
I sit with the lights off among shadows and peace
and the phone on the windowsill like a surly cat.

I am trapped in a courtroom of my own making,
hauled up before the judge, found guilty as hell,
sentenced to receiving no phone calls for twenty years.

Red Dungarees
For TVR and Nichola

‘Thank God,’ she said, ‘Friday, some music please,’
and she placed her bare feet on top of mine
beneath the table. She was somewhat hoarse

from shouting all day long, but a few drinks
soon put that right. I put ‘Abbey Road’ on,
it sounded great. George Harrison had died

the day before. ‘I think I may have to
buy some new clothes,’ I said, ‘and stop smoking.’
They were two things I’d never said before

and her eyebrows went up. I lit a smoke.
‘Know any shops that sell red dungarees?’
We sat there drunk and ha-ed and ho-ed and hee-ed.

Hot Glue

Who wants to sniff hot glue twelve hours a day? Not me,
I can't behave as if it was normal,
I can't sit down and switch the telly on,

watch a Clint Eastwood spaghetti Western,
spill beer on the carpet, how can I do any of that
sniffing hot glue twelve hours a day ?

I wake up and the house is full of cold water,
the same depth upstairs and down, also on the stairs,
I'm up to my navel in it.

It's odd how the cat breathes underwater,
how it behaves as if things were normal,
how its purring isn't muffled.

Big Turtle

It was definitely a big turtle,
definitely Colchester it was caught.
In a river, it had scoffed all the fish.

People have been drinking hard all weekend,
I know I have. Blues music clung to me
like smoke round a Mississippi camp-fire

and I needed a shave badly. Today
I need water, and a mission. I need
to find a way to make ends meet, sort of.

This woman gets paid to recline on her sofa,
cracking a whip while naked men do the housework.
"I could do that," says Stephanie.

Sofa Factory

I was following a series
of red-lettered signposts:
SOFA FACTORY,
and an arrow, pointing.
I was wondering
if it said SOFA FACTORY
on every street-corner in town.
Then I came to a yard
with some huge iron gates
and above the gates in red paint:
SOFA FACTORY.

The job was dead easy.
All I had to do
was stick sofa catalogues
into envelopes,
put an address label on the front
and stamp them
second-class postage paid.
I kept looking at the clock.
I kept looking at it
like I couldn't believe it.

There were four of us
at a large table.
The others were young blacks.
One of them asked me
if I was an alky.
He said I had that look
about me.
The other two laughed
and I smiled and said
I couldn't afford to be an alky.
Which seemed to be an answer
everyone could live with.

I Dreamed I Burst Balloons

I dreamed I burst balloons for a living
and was my own supervisor.
I worked twelve hours a week

and earned a decent wage.
I was never exhausted, never bored.
I was calm like a yacht

in a sunlit harbour,
calm like a rolling pin
or clay elephant.

My past life had been forgotten
like a dull episode of a cop show.
There were no scars on my body.

Nothing Nothing Nothing

1

You don't play football
with the rest,
you spend sports lessons
up a tree smoking.
You can see two of the three games
but you've no interest in them.
When they're finished
you can drop down,
mingle with the rest
jogging back to school.
There's smoke on your breath
but no one gets close.
No one acknowledges you
even exist.

During the dinner break
you smoke inside, hidden
behind some old gym equipment
in the basement, beneath
the head's office.

2

Eating baked beans
cold from the can
with your fingers
and your girlfriend's fingers,
sipping diamorphine
and cans of Skol,
the world's greatest harmonica player
could walk in the room,
you wouldn't act impressed.
"Scuttle along, fishhead,"
that's what you'd tell him.

You are so cool,
crawling to the toilets
with your girlfriend
riding your back.
It must take a lot of practice
to look so tough
in a leather jacket.
You'll keep the whole block awake
if you feel like it
and why shouldn't you
feel like it ?

3

Brooding in the bedroom
while the social worker
pontificates downstairs
with your parents.
You can hear the voices
but can't make out the words
and don't even try.
It's not long
before you are summoned.

You are in big trouble,
that's what they try to get you
to swallow
while you tap the chair-arm
with a biro, three-
four time.
You never shave
and have a kind of beard
which now and then
you scratch.

Not Pretty

The black coffee hits him like a slap in the face.
Slowly, very slowly, he colours in a picture
of the previous night. It's not pretty.

Some fresh air would do him the world of good
but taking a stroll's one thing he never does.
He'd rather put his fist through a window

or shoot passers-by in the legs.
He'd rather stare at a man's heart in a glass jar
on the top shelf of a shabby wardrobe.

He can't tolerate it, sweat running down his back.
'Just drink your damn coffee,' he whispers, then louder
'just drink your damn coffee and try to act normal.'

Our Monica

For Michael Massey

It's turned yellow, her left nipple.
She stares at it in the bathroom mirror.
She squeezes it, it doesn't hurt. Then

she's daydreaming about a place
where she can go for tea, where she's known as
"our Monica". It used to be at the end of the street.

She's been singing in bands since she was seventeen.
That's thirty-three years surrounded by men.
Drummers? Don't talk to her about drummers...

She can still hear her mother's loud, broad voice:
"She plays harmonica, our Monica.
Even at school she was always right musical..."

Sleepless

I woke just after one a.m.
to the familiar sound of a police helicopter
circling over the mill, down the canal.

Naked in the darkness, I stood and watched.
Something seemed to be taking place
beneath the thick, dark trees.

Well, the bastards had ruined my sleep.
I rolled a spliff, just a single-skinner,
some homegrown stuff, smoked it on the sofa

as the coppers hovered,
probing with their stupid spotlight
for any sign of life.

In A Heatwave

Twenty five to bastard seven.
A gathering of men in the canteen,
drinking murky coffee from plastic cups,

reading *The Sun* or *The Star* or *The Mirror*,
yawning and coughing and cheerless.
I take my place with them.

By eight o'clock I'm drenched in sweat,
juggling red hot rubber dog bones,
and by five past three I'm barely living. I turn

to the old black guy on the next machine
and tell him I think I'm going to die.
He shrugs - "Can't say I blame you man."

Against Suicide

People think up the strangest ways
to do themselves in.
I heard of a woman

who did it with clothes pegs.
Then there was a group of young men
who strapped bombs to themselves.

I won't be doing it
with bombs or clothes pegs.
I'd feel too self-conscious,

and I want to live long enough
to see the animated version
of the end of the world.

With the Bosses

The thought of engaging them
in conversation
makes my skin crawl.
Even so, here I am, speaking
and being spoken to
in a too-bright office.

Why is work always dull or hard
or dull and hard?
Why is there never enough time
to pursue things that make life worth living?

I don't ask these questions, just desire to.
I want to say I like the shift pattern -
four days on, four days off -
it means only half of your life is shit.

P For Poem

I'm tired, slumped in a chair,
struggling to take it in -

aircraft crashing,
buildings collapsing,

dust and smoke and holy shit
everywhere.

Things can only get worse,
I mean better.

Death's boots are shuffling
on the Welcome mat -

'I don't need anything right now!'
I shout.